M000198668

"We all make choices repercussions, and if we c to learn about our future Enter Ron James. After 25 years of incarceration he made the right Choices allowing him to re-enter society, and in *Living in Your Next Choice*, he takes you with him as he continues his inspiring journey."

~Robert L. Jolles, author of *How to Change Minds, The Way of the Road Warrior Customer Centered Selling* and *How to Run Seminars & Workshops*
President, Jolles Associates, Inc.

"As an Assistant, Associate, and Superintendent of Schools in three different states, and an instructor for seven different universities, Ron James' *Living in Your Next Choice* is a must read for all young people. If one can learn from another experience, this is the story that can change lives!"

Harry E. Hoffer, Sr. Ph.D.
Upward Bound Program Manager
DTCC Terry Campus
Workforce Development and Community Education

"I first met Ron James a couple of years ago. He had asked my wife (and his former classmate) to listen to a version of his motivational speech as he embarked upon his new career. Having been in a business career spanning over 35 years I had heard my share of motivational talks. I was blown away by Ron's passion and message of redemption, positive action, hope and love. He was amazing! I bought 20 copies of his book *Choices* and gave them to all my friends and family.

Now in his new book, *Living in Your Next Choice*, Ron continues to expand his message by encouraging the reader to live a life that is truly meaningful and to create a lasting legacy that will inspire others. Everyone can benefit from Ron's message. Make sure that this important book is on your reading list and pass on copies to all people in your inner circle. They will thank you!"

Tom Dyevich
Princeton Medical Marketing, LLC
Princeton, NJ

"I met Ron for the first time when he interviewed me for a position a few years ago. He had a contagious smile, an encouraging word, a bold bear hug, and a passionate enthusiasm for life! He believed in me and I got the job. I see now that he was, *Living in Your Next Choice* by helping others into their next choice. After reading his book *Choices* and now *Living in Your Next Choice*, I am confident that anyone who gleans from his experiences (both positive and negative) will pro-actively choose to live in their next and also help others into their next choice."

Dwayne Petty
Business co-worker and friend
Harrisburg, PA

Living In Your Next Choice

MARY AND RANDY

By Ronald L. James

Prov 3:5-6

Living in Your Next Choice

ISBN: 978-1-945169-08-3

Published in Partnership with
Your Choice Publications
1245 W Princess St
York, PA 17404

&

Orison Publishers, Inc.
PO Box 188
Grantham, PA 17027
717-731-1405
www.OrisonPublishers.com

DEDICATION

To My wife Anneliese, for making my life vibrant, worth living and stable with a listening ear, and to our blended family, Kyle, Karissa, Lanaya, Mireya for believing in me and constantly providing wind for my sail.

CONTENTS

FOREWORD

By Dilip R Abayasekara, Ph. D, M. Div

"Transformation" is a word that is often heard but less often lived. In Ron James I see the living embodiment of what it means to be transformed over and over again. I had the pleasure of meeting Ron for the first time a few years ago when he was introduced to my Toastmasters Club. Ron made a very positive impact in our club right from the start. In a short time, he was elected club president, without the members knowing anything about his past. Ron took it upon himself to tell us, in a speech, about his dark past. Instead of recriminations, all Ron received were admiration for having the courage to share his story with us and applause at how he had gone about changing himself.

If you read Ron's first book, *Choices*, you'd know his remarkable story of transformation. This book resurrects some of the elements of his past but then goes on to articulate his next phase – "living in your next choice." In other words, here are reflections that challenge me and should challenge all readers to stop resting on their laurels, to stop lounging in their comfort zones, and ask the vitally important question, "What's next for my life?"

Drawing on my past experience as a speech contestant in Toastmasters speech contests, I can see how this "living in your next choice" works. Over the course of six years, I threw myself into speech competition in every kind of contest that was available to me. Fortune blessed me in that I won a remarkable number of competitions and lost only a few. On hind sight, I realize that in every case except for one, I considered each contest to be a fresh start and not a "given" that I would win. It didn't occur to me to rest on my laurels. The exception to that was my greatest and most painful defeat. That was when I expected to win the World Championship of Public Speaking in 1993, having placed second at the contest in the previous year. At the 1993 contest, I was not "reaching for my next." I was reaching for what I thought should be mine. The pain of not even placing in the top three in that contest taught me a life lesson – that we are called to continuously evolve and improve; that we never arrive; that the change we undergo in striving to become our best is itself the reward.

In *Living in Your Next Choice* the reader will find Ron at his best: frank, humble, transparent, inspiring, challenging, and purpose-driven. I am fortunate to be able to call Ron a valued friend. The world is fortunate to get this message from Ron James –- whatever the past has been, if you continue to "live into your next choice," the best will come!

Dilip R. Abayasekara, Ph.D., M.Div., an Accredited Speaker. He is author of *The Path of the Genie: Your Journey to Your Heart's Desire and was the 2005-2006* Toastmasters Past International President.

ACKNOWLEDGMENTS

To all my friends, mentors and accountability partners who push me to greater heights. Especially, Rob Jolles for encouraging me, not to rest on my laurels, and to get on with the next thing in life, Jeff Bortner for never judging me for my past but befriending me and always accepting me for me Dr. Dilip Abayasekara for taking time out to coach me and write this foreword, and Dwayne Petty for painstakingly plowing through and editing each and every word of this book with precision. Which lens a reflection of his true character.

And to the entire staff of Your Choice Foundation.

PROLOGUE

Recently, I took a few minutes to look back at the finished work of my first book, titled **Choices**.[1] Proudly I held my book high in the air and rotated it back and forth as I mused at the front cover and then the back cover. Leafing through the pages, I had this special feeling that could best be described as having my chest poked out at the world as if I were this Marvel Comic Super Hero that took on his arch enemy and defeated him once and for all. I had this strong sense of accomplishment. Yes! I was finished. I was empowered, with the thought of being an authentic published author. I felt extremely happy holding a finished copy of the book in my hand.

For me to have come this far was certainly a great accomplishment. I say this only because it had taken me years to pick up a book and read one from cover to cover. I had told myself in the 4th grade that, "I hated reading." The truth was, I was laughed at and made fun of by my peers. One day, my teacher asked me to come up in front of the class and read. I did so with apprehension and fear in my heart of failing. As I read,

---

1   http://www.ronljames.com/

my hands got sweaty and I could feel the perspiration beading up on my forehead. It seemed as if my world was slowly closing in on me. Nothing else mattered. All I wanted to do was get through all of this without any incident. Well, then it happened. I ran into one of those words – you know the types that are more than 4 letters. I was struggling with the pronunciation and I heard something coming from one of the students in the classroom that sounded like a tire going flat. I peered up over the book and spotted a few of my classmates snickering. That was enough for me to call it quits. I went back to my seat and told myself that, "I hated reading." No! I did not really "hate reading." As a matter of fact, I enjoyed learning. What I "hated" was being laughed at! So unfortunately, I did not pick up a book to read until many years later. I struggled with spelling, reading, and even knowing how to form a proper sentence...

Back to the present...my book was eye catching. The glossy colorful cover highlighted an array of different shades of reds that faded into a black background, which accented a picture of a world covered with multiple chess pieces. The chess pieces gave the depiction that the world in which we live in is full of endless "choices." The more I mused at the cover of my book, the more I started to see and understand. My cover told more than the story that supported its title, **Choices** and I began to question, *why?* No! I was perfectly fine with what I saw, and the title was (in my opinion) spot on! A simple question was brewing in the depths of my mind... *What is next?* Literally, *what IS next?*

On this particular day, I reflected back in time and began to realize the many hours that were dedicated to the monumental project of writing a book. I recalled sending a short, handwritten letter (from the confines of a dimly lit 10' by 14' cell, with concrete and steel all around me) to my mentor and friend Rob Jolles. The words, "I have finished" were embedded somewhere in the context of that letter. Prior to writing anything, Rob had challenged me (or in reality, encouraged me) with the quest to write my personal life story in book form. It seemed at one point that the book *Choices* was never going to come to fruition. I would sit down and write sentence after sentence, page after page, and notepad after notepad, until I had created a whopping 1,875 page biography of my life!

I had received my marching orders from Rob early on and was sold on the idea that, "writing was not researching, outlining or even thinking. Writing was writing." And now I was "finished." At least I thought I was…. Rob Jolles is a natural born coach. He was not just a coach. Like Tom Landry, Vince Lombardi, Bear Bryant, Joe Gibbs, and Joe Paterno, Coach Rob Jolles was a winner. He had an uncanny way of helping me celebrating my success, yet focusing on what was most important. If you understand football you will understand the Monday morning quarterback. While I was living in the success of my present win with a published book. Coach Rob wanted me to live in my next and focus on the next game. This in this case was my next book. My thoughts of being finished were gone.

The truth of the matter was I was just getting started. I had no idea of everything that went into the publishing of a book, but Rob Jolles[2] did. He had a number of books with titles like: "How to Run Seminars and Workshops," "Customer Centered Selling," and, "The Way of the Road Warrior," and was working on a new book titled, "How to Change Minds." As I look back, I see now what I did not see then, and that was steps towards the *next*. I was about to live in what I call, *"living in my next choice"*....

"Living in my next choice" was and is a process. The world in which we live in is built with processes and systems, and in order for me to fit in, I needed to get in line with a positive process that was amicable for me and our society in which I now wanted to live in. I had taken the time to write out my life story in book **Choices**. This gave me the ability to see myself for who I was in light of Christ and living towards selflessness. I saw that I had made very poor choices along the way. I hurt a lot of people. I stole from anyone and manipulated everyone that I had come in contact with. This included family, friends and foes. I had no regard for anyone other than myself. When I realized the things that I had done to others, and began to focus on the destruction and pain that I had caused others, I wanted out of that type of lifestyle. I did not want to "do right" to just get out of jail or the trouble that I was in. I wanted to be free of self and all the negative and unhealthy consequences it had caused everyone. I wanted to think, act, and be

---

2   http://www.jolles.com/

different. So, I intentionally chose to turn away from a life of self-centeredness to a life that serves others. I recall thinking that the only people that I had to help were those that were all around me. That meant my fellow inmates. Let me share this with you - and I mean no harm, but this was not an easy crowd. I was challenged as being a fake, and someone that would never change. Who was I to argue? My track record spoke for itself. Statistically, I was destined to repeat the same behaviors. However, when you have statistics vs. right choices, right choices trump or override statistics every time!

Sitting down one day in the day-room of SCI Camp Hill (a common area where the men would often play cards, meet to have fellowship, and sometimes just sit and have a cup of coffee to collect their thoughts), I found myself re-writing my book *Choices*. One of the men came up to me and inquired what it was that I was doing. He seemed to genuinely want to know. So we engaged in small talk, which led me to answer his initial question. I told him that I was, "writing my life story in book form." He said, in a sarcastic voice with a smirk on his face, "so, you are writing a book?!" I was not about to allow his perception of me to become my reality, so I remained civil as he walked off telling me that, "books are a waste of time;" and "especially ones that convicts write!" I chose to use his energy as fuel to inspire me to press on. I realized at this point that some would understand what I was about, and others would not.

So, I went on a quest to reach out to the younger generation, and those first timers in prison. I found that I was better able to help the men that were new into the system. I gave them guidance with the do's AND don'ts of prison life. I had been in and out so many times that I had become an authoritative source on the matter.

In prison there are certain stereotypes. One of those is that of the "wolf." The wolves are there to take advantage of everyone that they encounter (I should know, because I once was one). Then you have the "sheep." The sheep are there for the slaughter. They are gullible, vulnerable, and weak. That is until they become wolves by choice or by fear of being victimized. I was there to lead the sheep, as well as to turn some of the wolves into "shepherds," in hopes that they would help others as well. This was the start of my process.

Next, I chose to surround myself with people who chose to help me. A number of people began to invest into my life. There was former State Representative Thomas Armstrong of Lancaster County, PA; Chaplain Drew Deagler of the Montgomery County Correctional Facility in Eagleville, PA; Michael Booth, Pastor at Water Street Mission in Lancaster, PA; and Michael Brokenborough, Pastor of the Household of Faith in Ardmore, PA. These Godly men gave me a platform to express my feelings as I attempted to find myself. They became my mentors, confidants, and friends. I began to form other connections and friendships through letter writing. Organizations like *Friend Over Fence's* with Steven Sands and Keith Sultzbaugh, and *Letters from the Heart Ministries* from a special woman named Sister Thelma Brosko. Letter writing became an outlet for the day to day need to cope with the harsh realities of prison life.

Next, I started to read more and more material that gave me wisdom and insights on how to treat my fellow man, coupled with programs like Alcoholics Anonymous, Narcotics Anonymous (working the steps), Thresholds, and Reconstruction Inc., to name a few. I wanted change, and "nothing changes if nothing changes[3]." I went to Bible studies and church. I answered questions upon questions to anyone who wanted to find out about the change that was taking place in my life and any positive thing that would help them to change as well.

This process was molding me into my *next*. By making my "next choice my best choice" over and over again, I found that I was able to be helpful to others and myself. I looked at it this way - my life was a big mess. Like a ball of yarn all rolled up into a big ball. In its balled up state, it is not good for much (other than to keep someone's kitten amused). However, slowly untangle the yarn little by little (like we do with making one right choice after another) and we see that we have a strand of yarn that is now ready to be transformed into a sweater, a hat, or something beautiful. No matter what mess that we find ourselves in, by making right choices, and consistently making right choices, we will be on the road to *living in our next choice*.

Today, I have the pleasure of going into middle schools, high schools, colleges and businesses, where I'm able to share messages on an array of various

---

3   https://answers.yahoo.com/question/index-
     ?qid=20070422083943AAL4BwM

topics. When I go into a middle or high schools however, my message on **Choices** deals with topics like Bullying, Social Media, Future Exploration (talking with students about their goals, visions, dreams and aspirations), and Drugs & Alcohol, to name a just few topics. When I speak, it is my hope to reach as many students as I can. I believe that this is where I originally went off course, and would hope to gain the most ground with students at these ages.

I was at Southmoreland Middle School in Scottdale, PA, in October 2015, when I received a revelation. The message that I received blindsided me and gave me a new found understanding as to how I was growing into my *next choice*.

I delivered two presentations/assemblies. Usually, in a forum like this, I give a 40 minute assembly, with a 20 minute Question and Answer session. It was during the Q&A portion that I was taken aback. The students were very engaging and interactive with question after question. Then a brave young lady hit me with a question that triggered emotions that brought me to tears. She simply asked me, "what is your biggest regret?" I thought about her question before I shared my answer with the students. Then it hit me - I had robbed my mom of something. And that something was not material. I had robbed my mom of a son...

In the next chapter you will meet this incredible woman that I had robbed.

CHAPTER ONE

WHEN LIVING IN YOUR NEXT CHOICE IS WRONG

What a profound statement. How in the world could *living in your next choice* be anything but positive? *Living in your next choice* is setting things in order so that you do not become stagnate or complacent. Whether through hope, dreams, visions or process, *living in your next choice* allows you to see things in a much clearer sense so that one can, "Make Their Next Choice Their Best Choice".

As a young boy, I heard, "Good, Better, Best. May You Never Rest until the Good Gets Better, and the Better Best." These words played over and over again in my mind, and were verbally repeated to me time and time again by my mother who was better known to all as "Mimi." She gave it her all as a single mother, left to fend for herself and her five children. She never lost sight of faith that one day her son would become a man. Not just a man, but a man that the world would revere as someone who helps others.

To best understand what I'm attempting to convey, I'll share a few stories...

The first story that I'd like to share with you takes place during a difficult period of my life. Trust me, there are quite a few, while I was battling with a vicious drug and alcohol addiction that landed me in and out of prisons for 25 plus years (nearly half of my life).

Most of the people that you see or may even know, that abuse alcohol and drugs, seem to have tattered lives and it's expected that these individuals will make poor choices and find themselves in less than fortunate situations. For myself, at this point in my life, I had burned every bridge imaginable - family, friend and foe. No one, including my own shadow, trusted me! I was at one of the lowest and loneliest points in my life. Fleeting thoughts of taking my own life raced through my mind. Needless to say, I needed help. The word "help" was an understatement, and I needed an entire medical staff, with all the fixings, real fast. I was heading towards self-destruction, with no clue as to what to do next, and with really nowhere to go...

So, when I ended up on the doorstep of my mother (the one woman who had seen something in me, beyond all my mess), I was welcomed by her warm embrace, and told to, "come in and go clean up." You see, going 4, 5, or even 6 days without washing one's body, and staying up all day and all night, tends to have a story of its own. I was hungry, run down, and lonely. But the one thing that you will never be able to fight against is when someone believes in you and you just so happen to be their *next* (she gave it her all). After my mother fed me, she directed me to go to her room and get some much needed rest. I passed out from exhaustion, for who knows how many hours. I woke up refreshed, rested, and wondering what to do next.....

Living in my next choice while in this state of mind was very detrimental and dangerous for me and others who suffer from addiction. For those who don't understand addiction in its rarest form, I will do my best to share with you my own personal insights and experiences, so that you will have a snap-shot of the life of an addict.

Some may claim that drugs and alcohol have ruined millions of Americans lives, but I beg to differ. Drugs and alcohol were never my issue. My issue, like millions of others who chose to "do them," meaning "to do themselves," whether with drugs, alcohol, the misuse of prescription medications, sex, over-eating, hoarding, power-tripping, gambling, and even the workaholic, are all one-and-the-same. It all stems from 100% pure selfishness and/or self-centeredness. All that I was concerned with was "Me, Myself, and I[4]." I wanted to know how others could meet my needs, at their expense. And if they could not help me, and/or I couldn't get my way, I was onto the next. This was the wrong way of *living in my next choice*. I could care less who I hurt. For me it was all about serving self. *Living in my next choice* meant living for whatever I could get from you next, and anyone else like you

---

4   Choices, pg. 63

that I could take advantage of. The core of my disease, the crux of my problems, was self-centeredness. I was *living in my next choice* the wrong way.

So, back to my story…it was a no-brainer - when it came down to what I was going to do next while lying in my mom's bed. I was looking to serve self, and I received my answer. As I opened my eyes and gained focus from a deep sleep, I noticed the sun had poked its warm rays through my mother's bedroom window, and landed on the table next to her bed. Something colorful and sparkling, like a rainbow light show, caught my attention. It was my mother's wedding rings. To get a deeper understanding of these rings that were on her table, I need to share this. Mimi had held onto these rings with dignity. These were the only thing she had left from a 25 year marriage that went wrong.

To make this long story short, I grabbed the rings, placed them in my pocket without a second thought, and raced down the steps towards the door. I could already sense my next high. On my way out the door, I heard the calm sweet voice of my mother who was working in the kitchen, none the less preparing a meal fit for a king. Heading down the street I had one thing on my mind - to get my next high. In no time flat, I walked out of a local pawn shop in Philadelphia with a mere $70. And within an hour, I was broke again, busted and disgusted, with nowhere to go. I had seemingly burned the only life line to my existence.

Well, this story would have it that I landed back at my mother's house a week or so later. And, who in their right mind would think that it would be perfectly fine to rob the one person who loved and protected them in the womb for nine months, cared for them every time they had a cold, skinned their knee, found themselves scared out of their mind, under the covers in a dark bedroom calling for mom to rescue them away from the boogieman. Who would have ever thought that they would have the audacity to ever cross that threshold again? Well, if you suffer from *living in your next choice* for the wrong reasons, you'll see nothing wrong with what you're doing. Why? Because you are serving self and you'll do anything for self.

When I knocked on the door, it seemed like an eternity before the door was opened. The door swung open and I was welcomed in with joy, greeted with a smile, a warm hug, and a kiss. "Ronnie! Great to see you. Come on in..." It felt good to be loved. Mimi had her big Georgia peach smile that could melt anyone within an eye shot's distance. On our way to the kitchen, my mother presented me with one simple question, "Ronnie, have you seen my rings?" Huh! Talk about a deer in the headlights...

While dropping my head in shame, I found myself speechless. Mimi placed her hand softly on my chin and gently lifted my head (as if to make me proud). With her eyes glued to mine, she smiled and said, "I know that you took them. It's okay." The next words literally drove me back to the streets – "Well son, I guess you needed them more than me." You see, Mimi was *living in her next...*

The second story is something that all of us have seen time and time again. It has to do with our, "Oh so important cell phones," and how we are at times enslaved to them. Now don't get me wrong, our cell phones are a useful tool, and a necessity.

Cell phones have come a long way. Do you remember how big and bulky they were (LIKE THE SIZE OF A BRICK)? Today these devices, which are so much smaller, can do almost anything..., i.e. text, email, keep time, alarms, calendars, take pictures, record and play audio files, not even mentioning any apps. I find the possibilities endless. Oh, and surprisingly, you can even make a phone call from these devices!

Now, I have a simple question, "who invented the cell phone?"

Let's take a look...The year was 1876. A man by the name of Mr. Alexander Graham Bell[5] was one of the primary inventors of the telephone. He held more than 18 patents. The phone was part of his *next choice*.... Then in 1900, on December 23 to be exact, on the outskirts of Washington D.C., an inventor named Reginald Fessenden[6] accomplished a remarkable feat. He made the first wireless telephone call. And he was the first to transmit the human voice, via radio waves. That was his *next choice*... "Can you hear me now?"

Fessenden's work provided the foundation for cell phones and networks. In 1947 an engineer named William Rae Young[7] proposed that radio towers arranged in a hexagonal pattern could support a telephone network. Young, who worked under an engineer named

5   https://www.britannica.com/biography/Alexander-Graham-Bell
6   https://www.britannica.com/biography/Reginald-Aubrey-Fessenden
7   https://glacomm.wordpress.com/2010/04/09/douglas-h-ring-w-rae-young-phillip-t-porter/

D.H. Ring, led a team at Bell laboratories, which was part of AT&T at the time.

Young, Ring, and all those at Bell laboratories worked feverously to accomplish what I see as *living in their next choice.*

In 1973 a competitor made a bold and cheeky move. That competitor was Martin Cooper, who at the time was an executive with Motorola, which was one of AT&T's competitors. Cooper led a team that designed the first practical cell phone, it was called the Motorola DynaTAC[8], and it was 9 inches long and weighed 2.5 pounds. Notably, Cooper is credited as the inventor of the cell phone. Well, there you have it..... Was Cooper *living in his next choice?*

YES!! And in the grand scheme of things, take a look at the whole universe. Not just the cell phone, but how everything is interconnected. Nothing is without significance. Everything seems to have a *next choice.* From Bell to Cooper, to you and me, and anyone who has anything to do with anything. We all have the opportunity to *live in our next choice.* But, we want to see what is wrong with *living in the next choice.* So let's get back to the cell phone, and how I view them as being a distraction for everyone who is caught up with them, and *living in their next choice* in a less than positive way.

I was out with a friend for lunch. We were at a local pizza shop and we sat down to enjoy what I thought was some quality time to get caught up on old times. I looked around at the other patrons, some were

---

8   https://en.wikipedia.org/wiki/Motorola_DynaTAC

couples, others in groups, and some by themselves. I noticed that everyone had their cell phones out, including my friend and I. Then all of a sudden I heard what appeared to be an unfamiliar ringtone from a one of the people in the pizzeria. Whatever happened to the old fashion "ring ring"? Anyway, my friend and I both peered over in the direction that the ringtone was coming from, and in that instant, I made the choice to look at my cell phone and make certain that my ringtone was on vibrate. I did not want to have any distractions when it came to validating my quality time with my friend. My friend on the other hand picked up his phone and as fast as he picked it up, he placed it down. I did not give his reaction a second thought. Well, that was not until his phone dinged. I know the sound all too well. There must be a text, Facebook Messenger notification, or an incoming email. Okay, so what's the big deal? The big deal is that *living in your next choice* while you're attempting to enjoy the present can become very distracting. Not just for me, but more so for my friend. He seemed perplexed and lost focus with our conversation. Then he became apologetic, by sharing with me that he was sorry, and then went on to share with me what was taking place in his life. I was alright with this until the annoying ding showed up once again. *Living in his next choice* meant that he would need to leave the moment. I get it. This very thing has happened to me. Yes, I'm guilty of reaping what I've sown with others.

So, what is the solution to getting back on track? Sure it would be easy to say to my friend, and millions of others, who do the same thing, "please turn off your cell phone." The only problem is that the phone will be off, but the mind will be running on to the next thought. Those thoughts are: who, what, when, why, where, and how they can get to their *next choice*.... My answers may not be popular ones, but they work.

Let us say that this scenario plays out. You are out with a friend and he or she receives that distraction. *Living in the next choice* for you is to release them to take that call and/or to follow up with that jolting ding (notification). The worse thing to do is to sit there and have a conversation, with yourself that spirals down into negativity. Sitting there with racing thoughts of how rude that person is. This could very easily build resentment, which would not be healthy for them, and even unhealthier for you. The more logical thing to do is give them an out, and let it go the first time. If the dings continue, then offer to reschedule (if this will not impose on either one of your schedules). The other thing to do, if time permits, is to allow them the time to *live in their next choice* and share with them that you're perfectly fine with them taking that call or notification and letting them finish up so that they are able to join you in the present conversation. For the person who takes the call or notification, they would need to either ask to be excused, or if possible, bring that person totally into their *next choice*, by sharing what that call or notification was about. I can't count the times that I've been on the receiving end of a situation like this. However, if I'm the offender, I can tell you that when I bring that other person into my conversation, there is a sense of relief that I can see on the other person's face. And often times I've gained incredible wisdom and insight by opening up to others.

Understanding this chapter is vitally important. I would like to share one more thought to place emphasis on its importance. Have you ever heard of the saying "keeping up with the Joneses?" Wikipedia coins it like this: "Keeping up with the Joneses" is an idiom, in many parts of the English-speaking world referring to the comparison to one's neighbor as a benchmark for social class or the accumulation of material goods. To fail to "keep up with the Joneses" is perceived as demonstrating socio-economic or cultural inferiority[9].

So, here we are. *Living in our next choice* and finding ourselves falling short when *living in our next choice* seems to be wrong. Harry Truman once said, "...America was not built on fear. America was built on courage, on imagination and an unbeatable determination to do the job at hand[10]." Millions of American get up at the crack of dawn and go to work. Others go in to work for a 2nd or 3rd shift. All of them work hours upon hours to get the job done. We American's take pride in hard work. And at the end of our work week we want to get paid. We take those paychecks and do whatever it is that we want with our monies. And for most of us, that means we pay our bills. My wife Annie calls it "Exchange Day." We take our money and it is exchanged from our hands to others. No big deal, as long as there is some kind of balance with the entire system. It gets messy, though, when we live beyond our means. And that's when "Keeping up with the Joneses" is dangerous for anyone who falls into the trap.

Let's take a look. For some reason we are all on this never-ending treadmill like a gerbil. It is January 1st, and we have celebrated another fine year. A late night, or early morning, in most cases, and it doesn't take long to see that you are already in debt. This takes place well before the New Year. As you view your bank statement (on your phone's latest app), you get sick as you notice the amount of money that it will take to pay all this off. January is almost gone when you realize that something else is around the corner. Whether it's New Year's, or New Year's Eve, or any holiday in between, we're stuck in a cycle. We go round and round every year spending hundreds upon thousands of dollars on things which seem to be so important at that time, but later, we find them collecting dust in some of the most secret places of our homes. These things, which at times are unnecessary, seem to serve only one purpose. That purpose is to "keep up with the Joneses," or *living in our next choice* for the wrong reasons.

So, where do we find that balance of working hard and enjoying life doing things that make us happy? I feel that everyone needs to search within themselves as they look for their purpose in life. For myself, I find that balance in helping others. If "keeping up with the Joneses" means falling back for the James family, I will not do it.

CHAPTER TWO

LIVING IN THE PRESENT

The following are a few of the quotes that I've found among the thousands of quotes that are out there on the internet. These quotes about living in one's present seem to drive home what I'm about to share:

- *The secret of health for both mind and body is not to mourn for the past, worry about the future, or anticipate troubles, but to live in the present moment wisely and earnestly.* **Buddha**[11]

- *One of the most tragic things I know about human nature is that all of us tend to put off living. We are all dreaming of some magical rose garden over the horizon – instead of enjoying the roses that are blooming outside our windows today.* **Dale Carnegie**[12]

- *Therefore do not worry about tomorrow, for tomorrow will worry about itself. Each day has enough trouble of its own.* **Matthew 6:34, New International Version (NIV) The Bible**[13]

---

11   http://thinkexist.com/quotation/the_secret_of_health_for_both_
      mind_and_body_is/147332.html
12   http://www.quotes.net/quote/3794
13   https://www.biblegateway.com/passage/?search=Mat-
      thew+6%3A34

- *It is a mistake to look too far ahead. The chain of destiny can only be grasped one link at a time.* **Sir Winston Churchill**[14]

These quotes are spot on! They are inspiring each of us to seize the moment. Now, what could possibly be wrong about following the wisdom and prescriptions that could lead us to success? Note - they all hold true to wise living. Although if not used with balance, one could find themselves very much stuck in a betwixt, going nowhere. I will explain...

Before I chose to take the plunge into my present *next choice*, which was a continuation in my life as an Author, Choices Life Coach and Motivational Speaker, I worked at Water Street Mission[15] (WSM) in Lancaster, PA. Most would consider this to be, at first glance, a rescue mission or homeless shelter. Well, it is much more than that!

WSM has been serving its community and many other surrounding communities, for over 100 years. They have adopted a philosophy to, "give a person a hand up, not just a hand out." The thought is to restore the person's life and help them to build a new mindset that would encourage them to break the cycle of homelessness and addiction. This process is done by identifying each individual's needs on a case by case basis. Each client takes a self-assessment that helps them to discover what their needs are and WSM partners up with the individual by assigning them a Case Manager and Life Coach. Together, the team helps to encourage, inspire, and hold the client/guest

---

14   http://www.quotationspage.com/quote/2582.html
15   https://wsm.org/

accountable to the goals that were discovered though their self-assessment.

Each client has an ongoing 30 day review that is used as a plumb line to measure their progress. This recipe is successful, unless the client allows the destroyer to enter in. That destroyer is named COMPLACENCY.

Yes, complacency would show its ugly face time and time again, and many of our clients would fall victim to its whims. It would seem that when a client would show up on the door steps, they were broken, tired, hungry, and willing to do "whatever it took" to get things back in order. Then, all of that energy that gave them the "fight for their life" attitude went out of the window once they got to a place that seemed to not require them to change. They were stuck in the present and the presence of complacency. Living with the hope to go to greater heights than where they were at seemed to die.

Whether we want to admit it or not, many of us suffer from this same type of situation. Complacency sets in and we settle with whatever it is that life has for us. Our drive to move forward is abandoned for whatever the cause. Some will argue that they don't like change. I get it. No one wants to live in constant change and the unexpected. But that is what life is all about. We are living in a world that is constantly evolving.

CHAPTER THREE

FEAR

The famous quote, "A mind is a terrible thing to waste[16]," was part of a campaign slogan used by the United Negro College Fund in 1972, to drive home the point of the necessity of education. Well, I whole-heartedly agree. The mind is incredible, and to figure one's mind out would be mind-blowing. And when it comes to the word Fear, the mind is that place where fear resides.

I heard it once said that, "faith and fear cannot exist together[17]." Well, not at least with the same person in the same thought. You are locked into one or the other. It works like this - thoughts race into your mind over the course of a day. Let's go over a few common thoughts to prove my point. You are on your way to work and the rush-hour traffic is normal. Yes, it's backed-up. You're about 20 minutes away from the office, and the traffic comes to a dead stop. You should have taken the alternate route when your GPS notification on your cell phone warned you that there was an accident less than a mile ahead. Then, all of a sudden you glance at the billboard that is directly in front of you and notice a young lady holding

---

16 http://www.adcouncil.org/Our-Campaigns/The-Classics/United-Negro-College-Fund

17 https://gotquestions.org/faith-vs-fear.html

a small little girl. You comfortably blank out, with only pleasing thoughts about your own daughter. You quickly respond with a smile. How lovely. Nothing else in the world matters. This is your baby girl that you're thinking about. You go into this daydream about how beautiful she is and how you have been there for her from day one. You were there for her in the delivery room when your wife gave that final push and she emerged into the world. You looked into her precious eyes for the first time. Your drove her home to your castle and placed her into her crib that you spent six hours putting together. You wondered why that same crib was left with nine extra pieces (this somehow becomes a theme when you build things). But, none the less, you were a proud dad that day. You then think about how lovely she looked in that rose colored tulle dress the day of her 5rd grade Spring concert. You recall all of the fuss that your wife went through when picking it out. She had only traveled around town and in and out of five different department stores to find the "perfect" dress, but it was well worth it. Your daughter was stunning, simply breathtaking. You ended that night by handing your daughter a bouquet of flowers and taking her and her friends to get ice cream. You think to yourself that you're a good dad. You see yourself taking pictures at your daughter's prom, visiting a number of colleges to help her pursue her career, and even walking her down the aisle to give her away, in holy matrimony. Your life is set...

Your pleasant thoughts come to a screeching halt when you hear a horn blowing. You look into your rearview mirror and directly behind you there is an angry commuter who is rushed and has his hand raised high in the air. Your thoughts are now focused on him when you realize that, we all have somewhere to go. But you get the point, and attempt to be more mindful.

You begin moving again and your mind settles back into the thoughts about your daughter. And just like the wind, your thoughts shift directions. You quickly remember that today is the day of your daughter's soccer game, and you have to show up and bring her home. No big deal right? Wrong! You are double booked! It just occurred to you that your boss is counting on you to stay late tonight. Your boss asked you to deliver the goods on one of the company's biggest accounts. Things should work out because you are well prepared. Plus, the field is only 20 minutes away from the office.

Well, unbeknownst to you, fear is about to show its ugly face and change your mood. You wonder how traffic is going to be later in the day. Your wife has made it very clear how important this game is to your daughter. You know that you have dropped the ball not just once, but twice before, when you showed up late to pick her and the neighbor's daughter up for soccer practice. You know how upset your baby girl will be if she looks over at the sideline and you are nowhere in sight. You've heard of stories of adjudicated youth who've shared their stories of how their parents never showed them that they cared; or how they, "only wanted someone to be there" for them. You then take note of your daughter's lack of focus around the house, and with you.

Then it hits you, maybe she is getting high. She even wanted to quit soccer early on. You have been spending too much time at work and away from the family. You think to yourself that you're a terrible dad. You see your sweet little daughter getting hooked on drugs and alcohol, you see yourself visiting her in rehabs and later on in prison, and even walking her down the aisle at her funeral as you carry her casket. Your life is ruined...

So how do we get away from the fear factor and its "doom and gloom" onslaught attack? The answer is a simple one. But before we go there, I can certainly share with you what I believe will NOT work - if you attempt to NOT think about a thought, it turns out that the thought becomes even stronger. Try it. Stop and think about something that you fear. I mean something that is bothering you personally, even at this present moment. Now that that thought is in your mind, do me a favor and stop thinking about it. How did you make out? If you are anything like me, now that the thought is lodged into my present thinking, it is all but impossible to turn it off!

So, what will work? Should we turn to willpower? Willpower certainly has its place. But even on a good day, the Willpoweroligist will give in and fear will creep back in. What will work every time is if I take that thought and place it *into my next choice* with positive thinking. "Finally, brethren, whatsoever things are true...honest...just...pure...lovely...of a good report; ...think on these things." Philippians 4:8 King James Version (KJV)[18]

---

18   https://www.biblegateway.com/passage/?search=Philippi-ans+4%3A8&version=KJV

Our imagination is something that we should use, and use it well. *Living in your next choice* when fear is involved, means to think on the next positive thought. Travel down that road, thought after thought, thinking on what could go right, and not on what could go wrong.

CHAPTER FOUR

HOW TO FIND YOUR NEXT CHOICE

❝We are treasure chests with more jewels inside than we can imagine." Ifeanyi Enoch Onuoha[19] Nothing is impossible, the word itself says "I'm possible"! Audrey Hepburn[20]

"Your network determines your net worth."[21]

I was once told a story about two cats -

There was an old wise cat and a small kitten in an alleyway. The old cat saw the kitten chasing its tail and asked:

"Why are you chasing your tail?"

To it the kitten replied:

"I've been attending cat philosophy school and I have learned that the most important thing for a cat is

---

19   http://www.goodreads.com/quotes/1037893-we-are-treasure-chests-with-more-jewels-inside-than-we

20   https://www.brainyquote.com/quotes/quotes/a/audreyhepb413479.html

21   https://henryukazu.wordpress.com/2014/04/16/your-network-determines-your-networth/comment-page-1/

happiness, and that happiness is my tail. Therefore, I am chasing it: and when I catch it, I shall have happiness forever."

Laughing, the wise old cat replied:

"My son, I wasn't lucky enough to go to school, but as I've gone through life, I too have realized that the most important thing for a cat is happiness, and indeed that it is located in my tail. The difference I've found though is that whenever I chase after it, it keeps running away from me, but when I go about my business and live my life, it just seems to follow after me wherever I go." Wayne Dyer[22]

This leads me to another story that I hope you will appreciate. It's the story of how I met my wife.

While spending nearly 25 years of my life going in and out of prison, it's obvious that a lot of my time was spent around other men. So when I mentioned to my coworker, mentor, and friend John, that I truly enjoyed his company and spending time working together, nights out dining, going to movies and countless hours of fellowship, but I wanted him to know that it was time for me to spend some time with the opposite sex, he understood. I shared this thought with other friends and what was said to me was that I needed to, "wait on God;" "be patient;" and "maybe it was not meant to be." "Meant to be" or not, I was on a mission to find that "special someone." I was *living in my next choice.*

Before I can go any further I would like to give you some background about my friend and mentor John... He is a very passionate person as well. If he believes in someone or something, he goes all out. So, when he saw me heading down the wrong path with my choices of dating, he had no problem sharing his feelings with me. He suggested that I try an online dating service. I was all in for his advice, but there was one problem - you need to have a credit card, and this was something that was not established at this point in my life. Being fresh out of prison, with no credit, I was not in any position to subscribe to any of the worthwhile sites. I tried the freebies and got all kinds of disappointments. They say that "you get what you pay for," and in this case I was not getting anything. You get my point? John came to my rescue as he has done many times before. He has done this for me and countless others time and time again. His life's passion is for others to be happy. John simply walked up to my desk, tossed over his credit card, and told me to "get the job done." He wanted me to go and set up an account with one of the more popular dating sites. With all of the choices, choices, and more choices, what was a guy to do? I landed with Christian dating website. I filled out all of my contact information and the profile that was required, and at the end of the day I felt hopeful and encouraged.

Several days went past without any real connections. At this point I decided to step up my game. I wanted to be creative and come up with something unique that I felt would woo that special person. So I came up with an introduction line that went something like this:

I'm a very warm and outgoing man who never judges a person because of their past. I have an ear open and a heart that is willing to do God's will. I love to have fun and meet people. I'm bright, optimistic, and a fun person to spend time with. I am like a coconut. I'm dark and kind of rough on the outside; however, if you take time to get to know me and are willing to work to find out what's on the inside, you'll find that I'm very sweet (how could I possibly go wrong with a line like this?).

Well, this very sweet woman thought that what I shared was very funny, and later I found out that it actually made her laugh. We began to correspond via the onsite email system. I felt that we should use our own emails and I was ready to talk with her on the phone. However, this young lady wanted to move a little slower and keep building our relationship at a much slower speed than I wanted. Since I knew that my way of doing things had created issues for me in the past, I was not about to mess this one up. So, I chose to slow down, and we moved at her pace.

One evening, while I was settling in from a long day at work, my cell phone rang unexpectedly. I noticed that the caller had blocked their number. As a norm, I do not answer these calls and just let them float into my voice mail (this way I can screen my calls). Well, for some reason I reluctantly took the call and what I got was an ear full...

I did not recognize the woman's voice on the other end. She was speaking fast and seemed to be upset about something. After listening to her I could make out that she wanted me to know that she was not one of these women who was going to stand for someone's "B-S", or any of my shenanigans. Later, after she calmed down, I was able to make out that it was Annie, the young lady that I was corresponding with through the website. She wanted me to know that she had finally given in to my wish to communicate via email, and that she had mistakenly sent me an email with all of her contact information on it. Annie was fearful that I might be one of these guys who stalk innocent women from out of the country. Later, we were able to laugh and for some reason this helped to give us a great starting point. We stayed on the phone for three plus hours that night, talking, laughing, and getting to know each other. It was at this point that I decided to share with Annie about my past. I wanted her to know right from the very start about my past...

I shared openly with her, no holds barred, that I was an ex-felon who just got out of prison and was still on parole and had a vicious drug and alcohol problem that spanned over nearly half of my life. Now, who in their right mind would tell a woman that they are attempting to woo anything close to something like this? Well, I had nothing to lose and everything to gain!

The phone went silent for what seemed to be an eternity. The next words that I heard were, "well, I'm certain that we can be friends." Friends?! I was looking for a wife and someone that I could spend the rest of my life with. If this was meant to be, then I had done my part and I was open and honest.

I shared with Annie that I had just finished writing my life story in book form; and, if she was not afraid to look deeper into my life, then I was willing to share it with her in its raw form (my book **Choices** had not yet been published). I sent her two chapters and she read them and then wanted the entire book. She read my book in three days - long before we even met! The funny thing about all of this is that I had shared with my friend John that, "the woman that would marry me would have to read my book before we meet."

Annie and I continued to spend countless hours on the phone. When we finally met, it seemed as though we had known each other for a lifetime.

Today, Annie and I share so much together. She willingly said, "I do," and we have a beautiful home and blended family with four children (including a little baby girl that made her debut two years later) and one granddaughter. We certainly share happiness together. Today, I find my joy and happiness by being me. By being me, I find myself able to help others.

CHAPTER FIVE

LIVING IN YOUR PAST OR YOUR FUTURE

Attempting to live in your past or your future - neither is practical. In both of these cases, it is virtually impossible to seize the moment - if our minds are tied up worried about what has taken place in the past; and/or trying to control one's future.

Mother Teresa put it this way: *"Yesterday is gone, tomorrow has not yet come. We have only today, let us begin."[23]*

Aviator, Beryl Markham in the book, "West with the Night" quotes: *"I have learned that if you must leave a place that you have lived in and loved and where all your yesteryears are buried deep, leave it any way except a slow way, leave it the fastest way you can. Never turn back and never believe that an hour you remember is a better hour because it is dead. Passed years seem safe ones, vanquished ones, while the future lives in a cloud, formidable from a distance."[24]*

This quote says it all so plain: *"Don't cry over the past,*

---

23   http://www.quotes.net/quote/50085
24   https://www.goodreads.com/author/quotes/1054.Beryl_Markham

it's gone. Don't stress about the future, it hasn't arrived. Live in the present and make it beautiful." Anonymous [25]

Then there is reality! As much as I want to go back in time to right the wrongs of all those I've hurt, harmed, or caused to have resentment towards me, I can't! To this day, I have no way of knowing all the damage I've done, let alone all of the people I've wronged…

I recall early in my criminal lifestyle, a detective came up to me after I had been served a warrant for a forgery that I had committed. He first wanted to know why I had done what I had. Then, with a very sincere look on his face, he shared with me some disturbing news. He wanted me to know that this particular store that I had stolen thousands of dollars in merchandise from, with my stolen checks, was "forced to close the doors to their business." He went on to say that, "they had been struggling, and what you did broke both their pockets and their spirits." I regretted doing that and countless other crimes against society in general; sadly, it was not enough to stop me from continuing to live in that self-centered lifestyle.

I share this next story with complete remorse because I realize that I took advantage of someone's kindness and drive to help all of humanity…

The young lady that I'm about to describe is and was an angel. We will call her Lisa. Lisa was a college student in her freshman year. She was trusting and wanted to help others. She had grown up following

---

25   http://www.verybestquotes.com/life-lesson-quote-8-dont-cry-over-the-past-its-gone/

in her father's footsteps by following principles from the Bible. She was independent and had her own car, apartment and was heavily involved with campus life at Saint Joseph's University in Pennsylvania. She had no idea that she was about to run into one of the most selfish individuals who had ever set foot on this planet. Yes, she was about to meet and have an encounter with the vicious Ronald James.

Well, I wanted to get high, but I had no money. That had never seemed to stop me before, so I went into what I call "clocking" mode. I ran this game, which went something like this:

The clocker would approach the victim whether at a traffic light, intersection, stop sign, parking shopping mall, or anywhere you could find people. The clocker would then share a story of their car being broken down and needing additional cash for repairs. They were counting on the victim handing over money.

Example

Clocker: Excuse me Sir/Ma'am, my car has broken down and I am trying to get to work. Can you help me please?

Victim: What is wrong?

Clocker: My fan belt is shot and I only have $16. I need $14 more to repair it.

Victim: Excuse me?

Clocker: I need $14 more to get a new fan belt. Could you please help me? If you give me your name and number, or business card, I can repay you.

Victim: Oh, that is not necessary. Here is $20 and I hope you make out all right.

This scam was simple and clocking went on 24/7 and you could not help but get paid. The best way to do this was to have a partner. So, I hooked up with this beautiful brown-skinned sister who, like me, enjoyed living on the edge. She reminded me of a younger version of my first wife, Gypsy (see **Choices**, chapter 4, page 91). She took nothing from no one, and knowing she was daring, I invited her to go clocking. I knew a female would add to the special effects and validate the scam that I was now running. The two of us headed up to the designated area in Philadelphia. It was late (around 2 AM in the morning) and this time of the morning always was good for traffic. After being out for a short period of time, we ran into some luck when our first two clocks produced about twenty dollars each. Our third attempt gained forty dollars. Then we met our young college friend Lisa. She was more than willing to try and help us. We told her our car had broken down and we needed money to get a tow. This young woman gave us money and her information so that we could repay her. We thanked her and left. As soon as we got back to our safe house, we got high. It was after my drugs were gone that I got the idea to "tap the well while it was still full." Meaning, "why not contact this young woman again while the getting was good?" I did not share my thoughts with my friend, I just told her to "come with me."

We made our way out the door to a pay phone and I gave the young woman a call. I could tell I woke her up. It had to be around 6 AM. We chatted and I began to tell her we needed $150 more to get our car fixed.

She was very happy to help, so she agreed to meet us. Upon meeting and giving us the money, she noticed my clothes had grease marks all over them, which was staged on purpose to make this whole encounter seem very real. She wished us well with our repairs and went on her way. However, I was not done. I created a payroll check, filled it out for several hundred dollars, and then called the young woman back. I shared with her that I wanted to come by her apartment to drop off the money that I owed her. When we got there, she was so happy to see us. I asked her to deposit my payroll check (which was absolutely worthless) into her account and subtract out what I owed her, giving me the change (which was around $400). She said she would, "run to the bank," and told us to "stay at my place, get cleaned up," and she "would be right back." She gave my friend some clothes to change into and I washed up. As soon as I was done in the bathroom, I walked out right as the young woman was entering back into her apartment. She handed me the change and I walked right out her front door. I was in the prime of my addiction, repeating the same old cycle. By the end of the day, I found myself back in jail.

When I got locked up, I would always put my thinking cap on. This seemed a suitable thing to do being that I had nowhere to go, and plenty of time to think. I realized a number of things during this time. First, I knew I needed help; and second, I wanted to go home. I knew I was in trouble and I quickly turned to God. I prayed for a few days and I felt very bad about a lot of things, one in particular was how I treated Lisa, who was special and truly had a heart of gold.

She did not deserve what I had done to her, and I felt compelled to call her and say something. I made a call to her, and when she answered, it took me a minute to get myself together, but I told her everything. She was not like the others that I chose to hurt. She had no ill intent in her heart. She did things for people out of her love for Christ and said her parents always, "encouraged her to reach out to those in need." Her actions proved every bit of what she claimed. After about five minutes of confession on my part, she said in a low defeated voice, "so the check you gave me was no good either?" I confirmed her fears by telling her the check was worthless. The phone went silent until she finally said, "May God bless you." I could tell that tears were running down her cheeks. If her tears had a voice, they would have been singing in perfect harmony with the tears that were now streaming down my face. My point in sharing this with you is that, "your past is your past" and for me to grow, I had to move on. As much as I would like to share with our friend Lisa who I am today, and how sorry I am for all the things that I did to her (and countless others), I need to move forward and forgive myself. If not, we could dwell on that negative energy that could pull us down. Please don't get me wrong. I believe in making amends whenever possible. This is something I learned in Alcoholics Anonymous. Making amends does work if you work it.

I would do a lot of thinking while I was in prison, and spend countless hours on getting out each time. *Living in my next choice* during these times meant getting out by any means necessary. I spent hours upon hours doing any and everything that was asked of me. I wanted to look good when I went in front of staff and later for the Parole Board. If it meant jumping through hoops and taking extra classes, or cleaning the dorm area to win favor with the guards, I wanted out of jail and that was the bottom line. Unfortunately, I worked very hard at getting out of jail, but put little to no time working on how to stay out of jail. That would have been my "best choice."

CHAPTER SIX

WHEN LIVING IN YOUR NEXT CHOICE FINDS YOU LIVING ALONE

I once heard it said that I should be, "doing the right thing for the right reason."[26] This was not always the easiest thing to do.

I have spent about half of my life in prison. If you have not read my first book titled **Choices**, I would encourage you to do so. While behind bars, I ran into so many situations that I considered gray areas. But then there were those situations that were vividly black and white. Once you stepped into either side, it was clear to everyone what you were doing. In many cases the person who stepped out of the shaded area usually was making a stand. In most of my cases, I chose what I knew to be right.

26   http://retreatday.com/meditations/the-right-thing-for-the-right-reason

You can see some examples of this gray area played out not only in prison, but on the streets, in our schools, the work place, and our families. Sadly, you find it on playgrounds all across America in the form of bullying. If we take a look at bullying for a moment, you will very easily see that there are:

- victims – those violated in/by the situation;

- perpetrators – also known as the instigators or "bullies;"

- witnesses - a person or persons who actually see the crime, but would rather not say anything because they take the stance that, "it's not my business." In some cases their thoughts are, "better them than me!"

Who would want to get involved if they knew that as soon as they stood up for what is right and exposed the wrong, they would then fall victim to bullying as well?

Then there's the whistle blower on the job who should otherwise keep his nose out of everyone else's business. Unfortunately, we find the bad cop or politician who is "on the take" (receiving kickbacks or favors). They would want others to believe that they are operating correctly; but in reality, they are duplicitous, two faced, and deceitful. If you expose them, they will soon hate you and find all manner of reasons to blame you or get rid of you. You are the person who is going to call them on their double standard and hold them accountable to the truth. In their eyes you're messing with their money.

On the streets there is an unwritten "criminal code of ethics," that if you choose to be a criminal, you had better adhere to. If you live outside of this code, and tell it like it is, you're called a snitch. The threats that are portrayed and carried out are typically extreme and violent. You'll hear sayings like, "Snitches' get stitches." Meaning that if you come out of the gray to do what is morally correct, then someone will hurt you or your family. Playing the streets could even bring death. You're told to "mind your business;" "turn your head and keep your mouth shut and you'll be just fine." As a matter of fact, to not say something is honored, and that person is seen as okay.

For the family it could even be worse. There are unaccounted cases of child abuse not being reported, where the family refuses to call Children and Youth Services. Other times there is violence from spousal abuse. The victim is ashamed, afraid, or feels like this is a normal way of life. They think that being treated "less than," is an acceptable way of living. The family, a religion, the fellowship club, fraternity, sorority, community organization, political affiliation and/or any groups can be so closely associated, that if you were to make an uncommon stand and merely voice your opinion, you may very well be ostracized, excommunicated, black-balled, or kicked to the curb and labeled an outcast. Not something that most of us are willing to sign up for.

Growing up, my father was a very successful businessman and an entrepreneur. At one point when we were living in Philadelphia, and my parents decided to move from the city of brotherly love, to the suburbs of Montgomery County Pennsylvania. We lived in a beautiful home, in an influential neighborhood, where I went to school with the children of doctors, lawyers, real estate brokers, and other entrepreneurs. We moved to this area when I was in the second grade. It didn't take me long to realize that I was different. I found myself being somewhat of an outcast, simply because of my color. I was the only black male in our school and the only other black person in the school was my younger sister.

For most children, all that is important is the ability to fit in. They desire to be loved and appreciated. So, when I was told by my fellow peers that I "walked" and "talked funny," I knew I had to come up with a strategy that would solve my dilemma. I changed the way that I walked and change the way that I talked. This worked perfectly, until I found myself visiting family and friends back in Philadelphia. They told me that I "sounded and talked like a white boy;" and asked me, "why are you walking different?" I found myself switching up once again to fit in. If you ever have found yourself on the outside looking in on a situation where others are looking at you as the odd ball, you know exactly what I'm talking about. It's certainly not a good feeling for me as I played the gray area only to avoid the spotlight of being an outcast or having the light shine on me as if I had done or was about to do something wrong. In my case, I chose to avoid being truthful to one-self. I lived a lie to please others.

This gray area is a very safe place for millions of us who find ourselves knowing what is right and wrong, yet we would rather live in the lie, or turn our heads to the truth by doing nothing!

I've heard it said, *"The only thing necessary for the triumph of evil is that good men to do nothing."*[27]

Living right and doing what's right for the right reason is what *living in our next choice* is all about. The more right we do, and the more we chose to step out of our comfort zones and stand for what is morally correct, we will ultimately benefit from our resources, abilities, experiences and strength and find ourselves helping others to do the same. This then becomes a lifestyle, and develops a mindset that breeds and cultivates legends and living-legends (like people that are famous in today's standard - i.e. Donald Trump, LeBron James, Queen Elizabeth), which change the course of the world in which we live in. This leads me into the conclusion of *Living In Your Next*.

---

27   http://quoteinvestigator.com/2010/12/04/good-men-do/

CHAPTER SEVEN

THE CONCLUSION OF LIVING IN YOUR NEXT CHOICE

What do Martin Luther King, Jr., Mother Teresa, Ronald Reagan, Joe Frazier, you and I all have in common? All of us have lived a life to be talked about. Now Martin Luther King, Mother Teresa, Ronald Reagan and Joe Frazier have all moved on from this world and on to their *next choice*. But, we know their names, and if nothing else, we know that:

- Martin Luther King, Jr., "had a dream;"
- Mother Teresa worked, lived, and served with the poor;
- Ronald Reagan was the President of the United States, or was it an actor, or both?;
- and, Joe Frazier could pack a punch.

My questions are:

- What about you and me?
- What are we known for?
- What will our legacy be?
- What will people say when we are long gone?

For myself, I would hope that people will talk about this guy who wasted 25 plus years of his life making poor choices, and one day the light got turned on in his head and what he heard went to his heart, then to his body, where he put wise choices into action. He finally got it, and he started making, "his next choice his best choice." But *living in our next choice* does not have to mean that we are famous. *Living in our next choice* should mean that our legacy has had an effect on someone else's life, even after we're long gone. Some of us hear the words of our parents or grandparents who have imparted their wisdom. Others gain inspiration from sports figures, entertainers, historians, entrepreneurs, pastors and officials. Others cling to those things from friends, mentors, and other family members. The point is, every one of us are here for a reason and we all have something positive to offer life.

This brings me to share a story that developed literally overnight. It's about my friend, Clay Davis IV. USA Today picked up the story by Gordon Rago titled, "Talks of improvement on night of Windsor Crash"[28]:

Henry Clay Davis IV and Ron James sat in a Hallam restaurant Thursday night, eating cheesesteaks and talking about life.

James, Davis' life coach, had met with Davis about once a week for the last two months.

---

28   http://www.usatoday.com/story/news/2015/10/29/motorcy-cle-crash-windsor-township/74834532/

On Thursday night, Davis talked happily about accomplishing one of the goals they had previously set - cleaning his room. It was "one of their best meetings," James said.

"We were really engaging and having a great conversation," James said in a phone interview Friday. "Toward the end of our conversation, he said to me, 'Should I be thinking about forgiveness?' I said, "absolutely, but that has to be at your pace. That's something we'll work with."

But after Davis left, driving away on a Suzuki motorcycle his dad had recently given him, the 30-year-old Red Lion man crashed. He was taken to York Hospital and died from his injuries around 9:45 p.m., according to the York County Coroner's Office.

Bad choices

It was Davis's father, also named Henry Clay Davis, who introduced his son to James.

Two months ago, at a parking lot in the shopping centers along Route 30 in West Manchester Township, James' car broke down. Davis' father, a 55-year-old who works in IT for Under Armour in Baltimore, was coming out of Alliance Computer. He noticed James and ended up starting his car with jumper cables.

He remembers saying to James, "I wish I had met you earlier. My son could use someone like you."

A short time later, he introduced his son to James and the two started meeting.

"He would share his dark side and some of the torments that were troubling him," James said.

The two "found common ground" when James would talk about his childhood, James said, because Davis could relate to having a rough time growing up. Davis's father acknowledged this too, saying his son, "grew to trust James because he felt like he wasn't being judged."

Growing up, James said he suffered from drug and alcohol addiction that took him on a "downward spiral." After going in and out of prison for the last 25 years, James turned things around. He recently wrote a book titled "Choices" about his life, and now talks to youth about his experiences.

On their last meeting, Davis's parting words to James were to, "drive safe and be careful."

James said to him, "You, too."

Hours later, the call came in from the police that there had been an accident.

Davis, who was wearing a helmet, was reportedly passing other vehicles in the area of Freysville and Stonewood roads in Windsor Township when he collided with a car, the York County Coroner's Office said. Speed was a factor.

Later on during the night of the crash, Davis' father spoke with James in the hospital. James was set to speak to a group of kids at River Rock Academy in Cumberland County.

"Clay said to me, 'Please share this story because my son made some bad choices,'" James said.

When he did share that message with the kids Friday morning, James said you could hear a pin drop in the room.

"I just feel like there's an interconnection with everything," he said. "That message was meant for somebody. That's how life is."

So, my point is this - here you have a guy who very few people in this world even knew. Yet his story lives on in the heart of those students that I shared his story with. I plan on sharing his story, and the story of his choices, as often as I can. *Living in your next choice* is all about helping the next person in theirs, wherever and whenever we can. The funny thing is that I shared with my friend Clay the night of his death, that maybe he could go with me on a one of my speaking events. This seemed to excite him and he told me that he "would like that." "I think that I will like that as well," I replied.

So what is it that we do to live life and live it in order to *live in our next choice* so that our lives mean something to our friends, our family, and countless others who come behind us for years to come?

The answer is very simple. But before I give you the key to what I call, "the Keys to *Living In Your Next Choice*," I would like to ask a favor of you. I would like for you to *live in your next choice* right now. You may wonder what is it that you can do right now to *live in your next choice*. If you're a father, spend some time with you children. If you're an employee, show up for work unexpectedly early and stay late to put in some extra time. If you're an employer, take some time out to listen to those who are employed by you. If you're a student in middle school and you see someone bullying someone else - whether by cyber, verbal, physical or otherwise, report it. If you're a person that just received a gift, then give a gift. What I'm looking for is for all of us to make the choice to go the extra mile to be kind towards others.

I want you to know that it took me years of living very selfishly and falling on my face countless times, going in and out of prison more times than most have gone in and out of the movie theaters, to finally get it.

You may have come to your own conclusion of what *living in your next choice* may be. However, for me, this is the key: I need to do everything (give it my all) so that I can to point people to Jesus and glorify God and help my fellow man whenever I can to be the best that they can, as if they were myself.

"Love the Lord your God with all you heart and with all your soul and with all you mind..." "Love your neighbor as yourself." Matthew 22:37 & 39 New International Version (NIV)[29]

---

29   https://www.biblegateway.com/passage/?search=Matthew%20
      22:37-39

ABOUT THE AUTHOR

A SOUGHT-AFTER SPEAKER and author, Ron James teaches, entertains and inspires audiences of all ages. His Toastmasters International speaking experience provides him with the ability to deliver humorous, yet to-the-point presentations. His words make the listener become emotional about what they are hearing; and therefore, think about the circumstances surrounding their own life, or the lives of people close to them. He draws on more than 50 years of experience (25 years incarcerated) to teach people how to make better choices. His programs on life events, coupled with a scared-straight approach to the harsh realities of prison, will open your eyes to a place that is becoming easier and easier to get in to, but extremely difficult to get out of. Ron stirs individuals to decide on better, wiser choices for everyday life.

Today, Ron's keynote speeches, seminars, workshops and training events attract many diverse audiences from elementary school students, to the 'Big Box' retail employees and management teams, and from parents to professionals. His book, *CHOICES*, was birthed as a way to inspire and help change lives.

Ron lives in Central Pennsylvania with his wife Annie, there new born daughter and their blended families. If this story has moved or inspired you in any way, let us know. We are here to listen to your stories and share in your life-changing moments because every choice comes with a consequence – we want you to enjoy fully the positive benefits that come with good life choices. Ron James is eager and willing to do speaking engagements and assemblies of any size. From keynotes, to Life Coaching, the content will be customized, delivered to suit your organization's special needs. Ron James will share his experiences with anyone – from the classroom to the boardroom – and workshops can incorporate small-group activities, role-playing, case studies, video, statistics, and in-your-face questions. Presentation materials include tailored situational stories and best-selling books.

To learn more about booking Ron James for your next meeting, training or presentation:

Visit www.RonLJames.com

Email Ron@RonLJames.com

Call 717-433-2551

Join Ron on Facebook: Choices with Ron James

AVAILABLE NOW

Choices is a compelling, inspirational autobiography that shares life-changing wisdom for anyone who wants to begin making better choices today. James chronicles the bad choices he made which resulted in personal cost and tragic results. His journey is a thought-provoking account beginning from a young age through his downward spiral which ultimately landed him in a nine-by-nine cell for over 25 years. James encourages and empowers others to learn from his mistakes. He challenges them to consider their choices and trust in God to experience a life greater than ever imagined. As you read *Choices*, you will discover the same truth James discovered. Choices determine destiny.

Retail: $23.95
ISBN: 978-1-945169-07-6

CHOICES BIBLE STUDY

This Bible Study is for you to dig deeper into the themes presented in the book and movie.
Retail: $10
ISBN: 978-1-945169-09-0

CHOICES WORKBOOK

This Workbook is designed specifically with classrooms in mind. Teachers can utilize this tool with their students in broaden the concepts found in the movie and book as our nation faces a critical epidemic.
Retail: $10
ISBN: 978-1-945169-10-6

CHOICES, The Movie
began filming
March 17, 2017

Please visit our website to learn more
about the movie and connect with us
on social media to receive updates.

www.ChoicesMovie.org

YOUR
CHOiCE FOUNDATION

Your Choice Foundation's goal is to enrich individuals
to build on their gifts to empower others.

Please send your support for this mission to:

Your Choice Foundation

1245 W Princess St.

York, PA 17404

717-850-3538

www.YourChoiceFoundation.org